A BUSINESS APPROACH TO GARLIC FARMING

I0430039

Complete Entrepreneurial Step By Step Guide To Garlic Garden From Scratch

ZHURI HART

DISCLAIMER

This book is intended to provide general information and insights on adopting a business approach to farming. The content within is based on the author's knowledge and experiences up to the date of publication. It is essential to recognize that the field of agriculture is dynamic, influenced by various factors such as market conditions, climate, and regulatory changes.

Readers are advised to conduct thorough research, seek professional advice, and consider their unique circumstances before implementing any strategies or practices discussed in this book. The author and publisher disclaim any responsibility for the accuracy, completeness, or suitability of the information provided. The book is not a substitute for professional advice, and the author and publisher shall not be liable for any damages or losses arising from the use or reliance on the information presented herein.

Individual results may vary, and success in farming enterprises is contingent upon numerous variables. The author encourages readers to consult with relevant experts, agricultural extension services, and legal or financial professionals to tailor strategies to their specific needs and local conditions.

This book is not intended to be a comprehensive guide to all aspects of farming, and readers should exercise their judgment and discretion in applying the principles discussed. The author and publisher do not endorse any specific products, services, or companies mentioned in this book unless explicitly stated.

By reading this book, the reader acknowledges and accepts the inherent uncertainties in agricultural endeavors and agrees to use the information at their own risk.

TABLE OF CONTENTS

ABOUT THE BOOK

A thorough manual for business owners and farmers looking to get into the garlic farming sector can be found in the book "A Business Approach to Garlic Farming." This book is significant because it offers a business-oriented and strategic viewpoint on garlic farming. Understanding the business aspects is essential for success in the agricultural industry, which is undergoing substantial transformations, including garlic cultivation.

The book establishes the scene in the beginning by giving the history of garlic growing, summarizing its goals, and describing why it's a feasible financial venture. The necessity of having a strategic perspective in the garlic growing industry is highlighted, along with the breadth and significance of implementing a commercial approach.

The book discuss the key elements of growing garlic. Prospective garlic producers can benefit from a basic grasp of garlic, including its kinds, requirements for climate and soil, planting conditions, life cycle, and frequent pests and illnesses. With this knowledge, farmers are better able to manage pests and cultivate their land, which ultimately leads to the venture's overall success.

The demand for garlic products, consumer trends, competitive analysis, and price strategies are all clarified in the market analysis section. For farmers looking to maintain their competitiveness in the market by positioning their products well and optimizing their pricing methods, this knowledge is crucial.

Farmers are guided in creating goals and objectives, risk management, budgeting and financial planning, and legal issues by the planning department. These components are essential to the long-term viability of a garlic farm, guaranteeing that it functions well within regulatory parameters and has a well-defined expansion strategy.

In-depth information on garlic farming procedures is also included in the book. Topics covered include fertilization techniques, planting techniques, irrigation and water management, pest and disease control tactics, and seed selection and preparation. Farmers now possess the know-how needed to cultivate garlic successfully.

A thorough explanation of harvesting and post-harvest handling is given, including when to harvest, how to harvest, how to cure and dry garlic, and how to store it. For garlic goods to remain marketable and of high quality, several specifics are essential.

The book delves deeper into the topic of marketing tactics for garlic goods, with a focus on branding, packaging, sales channels, and marketing strategy. Developing connections with buyers is emphasized as a crucial component, acknowledging the importance of networking and collaborations in the agriculture industry.

The book delves into organic and sustainable garlic cultivation, offering details on eco-friendly pest and disease control, sustainable techniques, and organic certification. This illustrates how ecologically friendly farming methods are becoming more and more important in modern agriculture.

"A Business Approach to Garlic Farming" is an invaluable tool for anyone thinking about starting a garlic farm or who is already in the business. It is positioned as a crucial manual for success in the garlic farming industry due to its methodical examination of all the different aspects of garlic cultivation, from planning and cultivation methods to marketing and sustainability.

CHAPTER ONE

GARLIC FARMING INTRODUCTION

WHY FARM GARLIC?

An essential part of the agricultural landscape, garlic farming makes a substantial contribution to both economic stability and the production of food worldwide. Cultivated for centuries, this fragrant bulb from the Allium family is well-known for its culinary use as well as its health advantages.

Garlic is an essential component of many different cuisines worldwide and is used extensively in both conventional and contemporary cooking methods. Garlic has been more in demand due to its therapeutic benefits, which extend beyond its culinary value.

There are several strong arguments in favor of planting garlic. First of all, garlic is a resilient and durable crop that can grow in a variety of climates. Farmers seeking to diversify their crop portfolios and reduce the risks associated with climate unpredictability find it to be a compelling choice due to its adaptability to a variety of environmental conditions. Garlic is also reasonably inexpensive to produce, which makes it a feasible crop for both large and small growers. Garlic is still in strong demand in both domestic and foreign markets, which increases its allure as a commodity that can be grown profitably.

EXTENT AND SIGNIFICANCE OF THE BUSINESS METHOD

Garlic growing has uses that go beyond its short-term financial gains. Farmers can generate multiple income streams from the versatile usage of garlic. The market for value-added products including garlic powder, garlic oil, and pickled garlic has been growing in addition to fresh garlic bulbs. Garlic producers can earn more money overall thanks to this diversification, which also guarantees the crop's continued relevance in several other businesses, such as the food and pharmaceutical sectors.

It is impossible to exaggerate the significance of the business strategy in garlic cultivation. A well-planned and strategic approach is essential to the prosperity and long-term viability of garlic farming endeavors. This entails being aware of market trends, refining farming techniques, and embracing cutting-edge technology.

Furthermore, using ecologically friendly and sustainable agricultural methods in garlic production is consistent with the increasing emphasis on responsible agriculture around the world.

By taking such an approach, garlic farmers support agricultural techniques that are socially and environmentally responsible as well as helping to ensure food security.

To sum up, garlic cultivation is a robust and profitable endeavor with significant potential benefits. It is an appealing option for farmers looking to diversify their agricultural portfolios due to its widespread appeal, versatility, and variety of applications.

Acknowledging the breadth and significance of the business strategy in garlic farming is essential to fully enjoying the benefits of this adaptable crop in terms of financial gains and sustainable farming methods.

CHAPTER TWO

COMPREHENDING GARLIC

GARLIC VARIETIES

Allium sativum, the scientific name for garlic, is a widely grown plant that has been valued for ages for its culinary and therapeutic qualities. A thorough understanding of garlic entails investigating several topics, such as its cultivars, climate, soil needs, planting and growth environments, life cycle, and frequent pests and illnesses.

Garlic comes in a variety of forms, each with unique tastes, textures, and storage qualities. Softneck garlic species are ideal for braiding because of their flexible stalks and mild flavor, like "Silverskin" and "Artichoke." Hardneck cultivars with a core woody stalk, such as "Rocambole" and "Porcelain," are distinguished by their strong tastes. Elephant garlic yields huge bulbs with a milder flavor; nonetheless, it is not a true garlic but rather a leek variety.

CONDITIONS OF THE SOIL AND CLIMATE

The climate and soil quality have a big impact on how well garlic grows. Garlic grows best in areas with mild summers cool winters and well-drained, fertile soil. Sufficient sunshine is essential for healthy bulb development. Although versatile, garlic thrives in regions with distinct growing seasons and is typically planted in the fall to allow for a vernalization period that aids in bulb production.

CONDITIONS FOR PLANTING AND GROWING

Garlic planting and cultivation require careful thought. When using cloves as planting material, they are usually planted two inches deep, with the pointy end pointing upward. Cloves must be spaced appropriately apart for the bulb to develop properly. Throughout its growth, garlic needs constant hydration, although overwatering should be avoided as this can cause rot. Mulching is frequently used to control soil moisture and inhibit weed development.

GARLIC'S LIFE CYCLE

Garlic has two unique periods to its life cycle. Garlic cloves respond to vernalization by going into dormancy throughout the winter after being planted in the fall. The plant starts to grow again in the spring, producing leaves and a scape. If the scape is left on, it produces bulbils that can be multiplied. The leaves start to turn brown as summer heat builds, signaling that the bulbs are ready to be harvested. To prolong storage life, proper curing and drying are required.

TYPICAL INSECT PESTS AND ILLNESSES

Garlic is vulnerable to illnesses and pests just like any other plant. Aphids, nematodes, and thrips are common pests that can harm foliage and lower bulb quality. Garlic crops can also be impacted by diseases such as downy mildew, rust, and white rot. Choosing disease-resistant types, rotating crops properly, and maintaining high hygiene are essential for handling these problems in garlic farming.

Gaining a thorough grasp of garlic entails investigating its various types, identifying the climate and soil requirements that it needs, comprehending the planting and growth circumstances, tracking its life cycle, and dealing with any problems that may arise from pests and illnesses. Garlic is a robust and adaptable crop that is still a mainstay in kitchens around the globe and presents special prospects for agricultural research and cultivation.

CHAPTER THREE

EXAMINATION OF THE MARKET

PRODUCT DEMAND FOR GARLIC

Numerous factors, including consumer preferences, culinary trends, and health concerns, interact to shape the market's demand for garlic goods. The popularity of garlic has grown beyond its culinary applications due to its possible health benefits. As a result, there is a growing need for supplements, oils, and other derivatives made from garlic. Growing consumer knowledge of garlic's anti-inflammatory and antioxidant qualities has made it a popular option for those who are health-conscious.

SHOPPER PATTERNS

How the market for garlic goods is shaped is mostly determined by consumer trends. Natural and functional foods are in high demand as people place an increasing emphasis on leading healthy lifestyles. There has been a surge in the demand for garlic products that are derived responsibly and organically, which is indicative of a broader trend towards ecologically conscious shopping. Consumption of garlic products has also changed as a result of shifting dietary choices, such as the development of plant-based diets.

ANALYSIS OF COMPETITORS

awareness of the competitive environment and seeing strategic opportunities in the market for garlic products require a thorough awareness of competitors. There are many different types of competitors in this market, ranging from big international corporations to small-scale local producers.

Marketing tactics, creative packaging, and high-quality products are frequently the main focuses of differentiation efforts. Businesses can improve their overall competitive stance, capitalize on market gaps, and develop their strategies by knowing the advantages and disadvantages of their rivals.

STRATEGIES FOR PRICING

The market for garlic products has a wide range of pricing techniques that take into account things like manufacturing costs, perceived value, and market placement. Specialty garlic products, including gourmet or organic varieties, are more expensive because of their claimed superiority and health advantages.

Price elasticity is an important factor to take into account because, although consumers might be prepared to pay more for particular features, excessively high costs have the potential to reduce demand. Strategies like discounts, bundling, and special pricing are also frequently used to draw in price-conscious customers and increase sales.

A wide range of factors impact the dynamic market for garlic products. Businesses must comprehend the factors influencing demand, customer patterns, the competitive environment, and successful pricing techniques to effectively navigate this market.

To continue growing and being relevant in the garlic product industry, companies must invest in product innovation, adjust to shifting consumer tastes, and maintain a competitive price strategy.

CHAPTER FOUR

ORGANIZING YOUR FARM TO GROW GARLIC

ESTABLISHING OBJECTIVES AND GOALS

A crucial first step in organizing your garlic farm is defining your goals and objectives, which serve as a guide for your business. Start by outlining your farm's overarching goal and vision. Take into account elements like the target market, production scale, and sustainable farming techniques.

Establishing SMART goals—specific, measurable, achievable, relevant, and time-bound—will direct your planning process's resource allocation and decision-making.

Aspects like yield targets, market expansion, or environmental sustainability may be part of your objectives. For example, you may want to grow a certain amount of garlic each year, hit certain sales targets, or use environmentally responsible procedures. Creating a purposeful and cohesive plan for your garlic farm will be made easier by matching your objectives with your values and long-term ambitions.

FINANCIAL PLANNING AND BUDGETING

Successful financial planning and budgeting are essential for any agricultural endeavor, including a garlic farm. Begin by listing all of the expenses related to starting and running the farm, including labor, equipment, seeds, land acquisition, and marketing. Create a thorough budget that details both variable and fixed costs, accounting for unexpected emergencies and seasonal variations.

To guarantee that your estimates are accurate and to investigate possible funding sources, think about consulting a financial advisor. When projecting your predicted income, be sure to account for future swings and the current price of garlic. As your garlic farm grows, review and update your budget regularly and be ready to adjust to shifting market conditions or unforeseen obstacles.

RISK CONTROL

Planning your garlic farm must include risk management, which involves identifying, evaluating, and reducing possible dangers to your enterprise. Examine all the external and internal elements that can affect your farm, including market fluctuations, pests, diseases, climate variability, and regulatory changes. Create plans to reduce the effects of these hazards and strengthen the resilience of your farm.

Strategies for mitigating risk include diversifying crop production, purchasing insurance, and implementing sustainable farming methods. Remain up to date on market developments and new threats, and take the initiative to modify your strategy as necessary. You may better position your garlic farm to handle uncertainty and ensure long-term profitability by tackling potential issues head-on.

LEGAL ASPECTS TO TAKE INTO ACCOUNT

When organizing your garlic farm, it is crucial to understand the legal environment to guarantee adherence to regional, national, and local laws. To make sure your selected place is appropriate for agricultural activities, start by investigating local zoning rules and land-use regulations. To reduce your farm's ecological impact, get any licenses or permissions needed for farming operations, and educate yourself on environmental laws.

In addition, take into account any applicable legal issues about contracts, employment, and intellectual property. A detailed agreement can help avoid future conflicts with distributors, suppliers, and other partners. To guarantee that your garlic farm stays within the law and promotes a foundation of legality and ethical business practices, speak with attorneys who specialize in agricultural law.

CHAPTER FIVE

METHODS OF GROWING GARLIC

CHOOSING AND PREPARING SEEDS

Carefully choosing and preparing seeds is the first step in garlic production. An abundant crop of garlic depends on using high-quality seed garlic. Usually, farmers pick bulbs from the crop that was harvested the year before, looking for ones that have desired characteristics like size, uniformity, and resistance to disease.

After selection, the bulbs are meticulously divided into distinct cloves in preparation for planting. Make sure the garlic seed is disease-free before planting, as diseased cloves can result in low yields and poor quality.

Some growers choose to soak cloves beforehand in a fungicide or garlic extract solution to further improve seed viability.

PLANTING TECHNIQUES

There are several ways to plant garlic, and which one to choose frequently depends on the environment, the kind of soil, and the available equipment. Transplanting and direct seeding are the two main techniques. Direct seeding is putting individual cloves in the ground at the right time of year. On the other hand, transplanting entails cultivating garlic in a different location before moving the young plants into the main field. To maximize plant development and enable effective harvesting, farmers take into account variables including row layout, planting depth, and spacing.

MANAGEMENT OF WATER AND IRRIGATION

Garlic cultivation requires proper irrigation since garlic plants need constant moisture levels during their growth cycle. To guarantee accurate water supply, minimize water waste, and lower the risk of diseases linked to excessive moisture, drip irrigation systems are frequently used. Farmers also consider when to irrigate their crops, since various amounts of water are needed during the early and late stages of growth. To avoid water logging, which can result in root rot and other problems, adequate drainage is equally important.

EMBRYOLOGY PROCEDURES

To increase bulb development and encourage healthy plant growth, fertilization is essential in the production of garlic. Soil tests are done before planting to determine the quantities of nutrients present, allowing farmers to adjust the amount of fertilizer they apply. It is possible to utilize both synthetic and organic fertilizers; the three main ingredients are potassium, phosphorus, and nitrogen.

Garlic needs a balanced nutrient profile, and growers frequently add organic matter, like compost, to enhance soil fertility and structure. Fertilizers should be applied on schedule, both before and during the growth season, to promote healthy garlic plants and higher harvests.

STRATEGIES FOR CONTROLLING DISEASES AND PESTS

Since garlic is prone to several pests and illnesses, it is imperative to implement efficient management measures to guarantee a good crop. Aphids, thrips, and nematodes are common pests, and diseases like rust and white rot can harm garlic plants. The use of Integrated Pest Management (IPM) techniques is common; these techniques include cultural norms, biological management, and if required, chemical interventions. Crop rotation breaks the cycles of pests and diseases, and choosing disease-resistant garlic types can add another line of defense. Frequent observation of the crop for indications of pests or diseases enables prompt intervention and the application of suitable control measures, hence reducing the need for chemical inputs. Overall, maintaining a healthy garlic crop requires a comprehensive and proactive strategy for pest and disease management.

CHAPTER SIX

HARVESTING AND HANDLING AFTER HARVEST

CALCULATING THE HARVEST TIME

One of the most important aspects of effective agriculture, especially when growing commodities like garlic, is figuring out when to harvest something. Several variables, including the crop variety, the weather, and the intended purpose, affect when crops are harvested. When it comes to garlic, the maturation and size of the bulb generally dictate the timing. Delaying the harvest may result in overmature bulbs of lower quality, while harvesting too soon may produce undeveloped bulbs.

METHODS OF HARVESTING

Selecting the right harvesting methods is essential to maintaining garlic bulb quality and producing a good crop. One popular technique is hand harvesting, which involves pulling bulbs by hand from the ground. Although this method requires a lot of work, it allows for a meticulous and deliberate harvest. An alternative is to use mechanical harvesters, which need a lot less effort when used for large-scale production. Although mechanical harvesters are effective, their precision may be inferior to that of hand harvesting, which could result in harm to the bulbs in the process.

GARLIC CURING AND DRYING

Garlic bulbs need to be properly cured and dried after harvesting to improve their flavor, shelf life, and marketability. Curing entails letting the bulbs dry for a few weeks in a place with good ventilation. The garlic bulb's outer layers tighten and dry during this time, improving storage quality. The bulbs are prepared for drying, which lowers the moisture content even further, after curing. Proper drying extends the shelf life of the garlic and inhibits the growth of mold. Using specialized drying equipment or hanging garlic bulbs in a well-ventilated area are common techniques.

PRESERVATION TECHNIQUES

To keep garlic's quality and market value constant throughout time, it is imperative to employ effective preservation techniques. It is recommended to keep garlic bulbs in a dry, cold place with adequate ventilation. The recommended temperature range for storage is 32°F to 50°F (0°C to 10°C). Garlic needs a relative humidity of between 60% and 70% to thrive, therefore controlling humidity is essential to preventing mold and sprouting. To promote air circulation, bulbs should be kept in mesh bags or containers with good ventilation. Additionally, to guarantee a longer shelf life and stop the spread of problems, it's critical to periodically check stored garlic and remove any broken or sprouting bulbs. To maximize the quality and post-harvest life of garlic, several storage techniques must be used.

CHAPTER SEVEN

PROMOTING YOUR PRODUCTS USING GARLIC

PACKAGING AND BRANDING

When it comes to successfully marketing garlic goods, branding and packaging are essential. In a crowded market, building a strong brand identity is essential to being seen. The branding should tell a distinct tale about the origin, quality, and distinguishing qualities of the garlic products.

This entails coming up with a catchy logo, picking suitable typefaces and colors, and developing an engaging brand statement that appeals to the intended market. In addition to being aesthetically pleasing, the packaging should guarantee the freshness and caliber of the garlic items.

Using sustainable and eco-friendly packaging can improve the brand's reputation and draw in customers who care about the environment.

FORMULATING A MARKETING STRATEGY

To direct the overall strategy and methods for advertising garlic products, a marketing plan must be developed. This strategy should include a detailed examination of the market, target audience identification, competitive analysis, and trend recognition. Important elements include laying out plans for product positioning, price, and promotion as well as clearly defining marketing objectives. The reach and impact of the marketing campaigns can be increased by utilizing both traditional and digital marketing channels, such as influencers, social media, and online platforms. A budget and schedule for the implementation of different marketing initiatives should also be included in the plan.

CHANNELS OF SALES

Garlic items can reach consumers through a variety of channels, known as sales channels. In addition to conventional retail locations, investigating internet platforms, farmers' markets, and niche shops might offer further routes for distribution. Forming alliances with supermarket chains or eateries can improve the availability and visibility of products. E-commerce systems provide a direct channel of communication with customers all over the world, enabling easy online shopping. A multi-channel strategy can be put into place to take advantage of various customer preferences and increase sales prospects.

DEVELOPING CONNECTIONS WITH PURCHASERS

One of the most important aspects of running a successful garlic product business is developing relationships with buyers. This entails being aware of the requirements and tastes of purchasers, be they wholesalers, retailers, or individual customers. Trust and loyalty can only be developed via consistent communication, gathering feedback, and promptly answering customer questions. Strengthening these relationships can be further achieved by providing returning customers with individualized deals, discounts, or special promotions. Long-term success and expansion can also be facilitated by attending industry events, networking with prospective customers, and looking to form alliances with important supply chain participants. In addition to achieving quick sales, developing great relationships with buyers lays the groundwork for future commercial partnerships and client loyalty.

CHAPTER EIGHT

ORGANIC AND SUSTAINABLE GARLIC FARMING

Organic Certification: Growing garlic organically requires adhering to sustainable and ecologically friendly farming methods. Getting organic certified, a rigorous process that guarantees conformity to particular rules set by regulatory agencies is one important part of this dedication.

Growers who wish to certify their garlic as organic are required to abstain from using artificial fertilizers, herbicides, and pesticides. Rather, they emphasize the use of organic substitutes such as crop rotation, composting, and cover crops to preserve the fertility and health of the soil.

Regular inspections to confirm adherence to organic standards are another part of the certification process, which promotes accountability and openness among organic garlic growers.

ECOLOGICAL METHODS

The foundation of organic garlic cultivation is sustainability, with a focus on resource conservation and long-term environmental health. Garlic is rotated with other crops as part of a basic sustainable strategy to stop soil erosion and nutrient depletion. Furthermore, cover crops are used to improve soil fertility, lessen erosion, and create habitat for helpful creatures. Another important component of sustainable garlic cultivation is water conservation, which is achieved by using techniques like rainwater gathering and drip irrigation to maximize water use. Energy efficiency on farms is another aspect of sustainable practices; it promotes the use of renewable energy sources and reduces the carbon footprint of growing garlic.

ECO-FRIENDLY PEST AND DISEASE MANAGEMENT

Rather than using artificial pesticides that can degrade garlic quality and harm the environment, organic garlic cultivation places a higher priority on eco-friendly techniques for controlling pests and diseases. The comprehensive strategy of controlling pests known as Integrated Pest Management (IPM) blends mechanical, cultural, and biological techniques. To organically control pest populations, beneficial insects like ladybugs and predatory beetles are introduced to the garlic fields. To reduce the need for chemical treatments, it is also important to cultivate garlic kinds resistant to common illnesses. The resilience of the garlic farm is enhanced by crop variety and the preservation of a balanced ecology, which lessens the farm's vulnerability to pest infestations and disease outbreaks.

Organic garlic cultivation represents a dedication to sustainable methods, organic certification, and environmentally friendly control of pests and diseases. Garlic producers support customer welfare, environmental health, and the general sustainability of agricultural systems by abiding by these guidelines.

www.ingramcontent.com/pod-product-compliance
Lightning Source LLC
Chambersburg PA
CBHW070843290526
45795CB00002B/968